Scary Creatures
SNAKES ALIVE

Written by
Penny Clarke

Illustrated by
Mark Bergin and
Carolyn Scrace

W
FRANKLIN WATTS
A Division of Scholastic Inc.
NEW YORK • TORONTO • LONDON • AUCKLAND • SYDNEY
MEXICO CITY • NEW DELHI • HONG KONG
DANBURY, CONNECTICUT

Created and designed
by David Salariya

Author:

Penny Clarke is an author and editor specializing in non-fiction books for children. The books she has written include titles on natural history, rainforests, and volcanoes, as well as others on different periods of history. She used to live in central London, but thanks to modern technology she has now realized her dream of being able to live and work in the countryside.

Artists:

Mark Bergin was born in Hastings, England, in 1961. He studied at Eastbourne College of Art and has illustrated many children's non-fiction books. He lives in Bexhill-on-Sea, England, with his wife and three children.

Carolyn Scrace is a graduate of Brighton College of Art, specializing in design and illustration. She has worked in animation, advertising, and children's fiction and non-fiction, particularly natural history.

Series Creator:

David Salariya was born in Dundee, Scotland. In 1989, he established The Salariya Book Company. He has illustrated a wide range of books and has created many new series for publishers in the U.K. and overseas. He lives in Brighton, England, with his wife, illustrator Shirley Willis, and their son.

Consultant:

Dr. Gerald Legg holds a doctorate in zoology from Manchester University. He worked in West Africa for several years as a lecturer and rainforest researcher. His current position is biologist at the Booth Museum of Natural History in Brighton, England. He is also the author of many natural history books for children.

Editors:

Stephanie Cole
Karen Barker Smith

Created, designed, and produced by
The Salariya Book Company Ltd
Book House
25 Marlborough Place,
Brighton BN1 1UB

Visit the Salariya Book Company at
www.salariya.com

A CIP catalog record for this title is available from the Library of Congress.

ISBN 0-531-14673-1 (Lib. Bdg.)
ISBN 0-531-14845-9 (Pbk.)

Published in the United States by Franklin Watts
A Division of Scholastic Inc.
90 Sherman Turnpike
Danbury, CT 06816

Reprinted in China in 2005.

Printed on paper from sustainable forests.

Photo Credits:

Anthony Bannister, NHPA: 13, 17, 23, 24
John Foxx Images: 15
Hellio & Van Ingen, NHPA: 10, 16
Daniel Heuclin, NHPA: 11, 14, 20, 25
Karl Switak, NHPA: 26
Martin Wendler, NHPA: 19, 27

Contents

What Is a Snake?

Snakes are **cold-blooded** animals that have dry, scaly skin. They breathe with lungs and have backbones. They do not have legs. A snake is a type of **reptile**.

Is a snake a reptile?

Yes, a snake is a reptile.

Is a crocodile a reptile?

Yes, a crocodile is a reptile.

Like snakes and lizards, crocodiles have dry, scaly skin and breathe with lungs. A crocodile's nostrils are high on its head. This helps it breathe and stay hidden just under the surface of the water.

Most **amphibians** begin their lives in water and breathe through **gills** before their lungs have fully grown. They also have moist, soft skin. Reptiles always breathe with lungs and have scaly skin. A frog is an amphibian, not a reptile.

Is a frog a reptile?

Croak

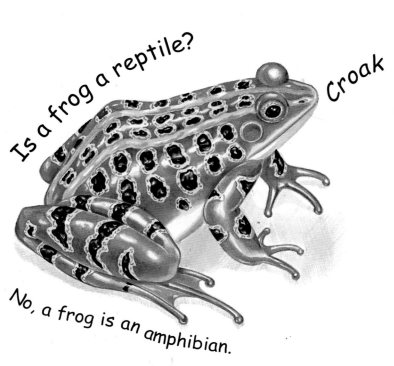

No, a frog is an amphibian.

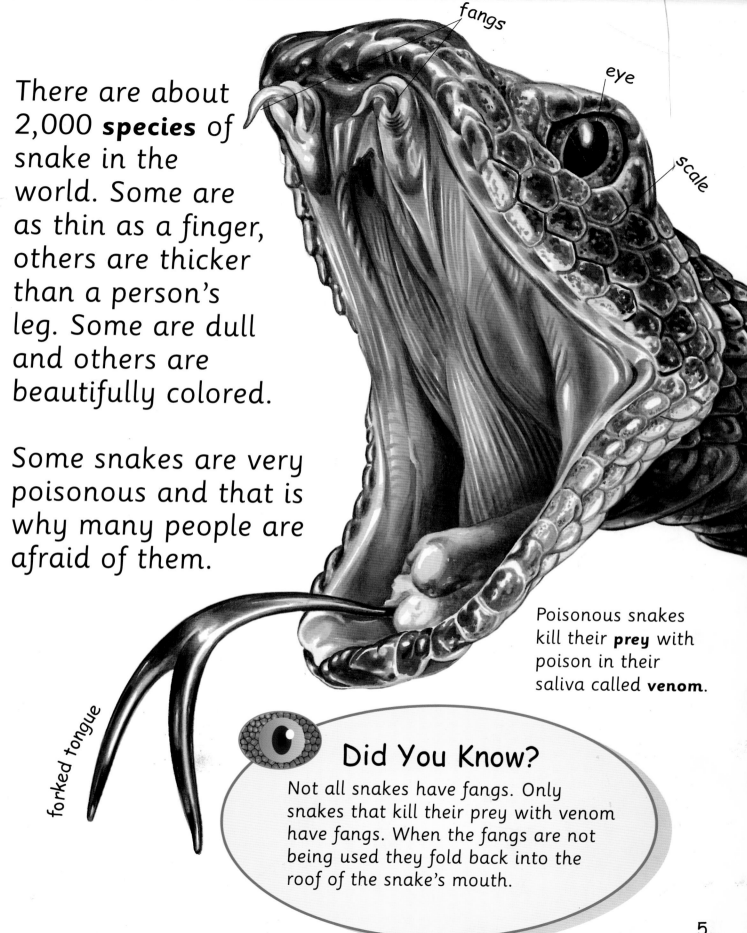

There are about 2,000 **species** of snake in the world. Some are as thin as a finger, others are thicker than a person's leg. Some are dull and others are beautifully colored.

Some snakes are very poisonous and that is why many people are afraid of them.

fangs

eye

scale

forked tongue

Poisonous snakes kill their **prey** with poison in their saliva called **venom**.

Did You Know?

Not all snakes have fangs. Only snakes that kill their prey with venom have fangs. When the fangs are not being used they fold back into the roof of the snake's mouth.

How Do Snakes Move?

Most snakes move in a series of curves. As each curve presses against the ground, it pushes the snake's body forward (diagrams 1 – 3).

Some snakes creep along on their stomach scales, pressing their ribs against the ground (diagram 4).

Rattlesnakes and vipers use another movement called "sidewinding" to cross loose, hot sand.

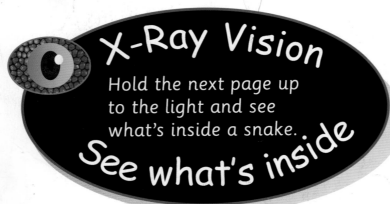

X-Ray Vision

Hold the next page up to the light and see what's inside a snake.

See what's inside

Snake movement

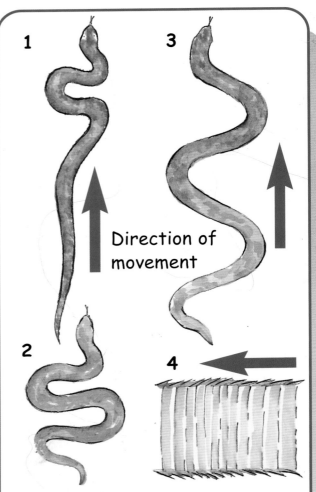

Direction of movement

1. Front end forms loops, then 2. the tail is pulled towards the head; 3. Wriggling curves – the outer edge of the loops grip the ground as the snake wriggles forward; 4. Creeping movement – the stomach scales bunch up and push the snake forward like a caterpillar.

overlapping scales

dry skin

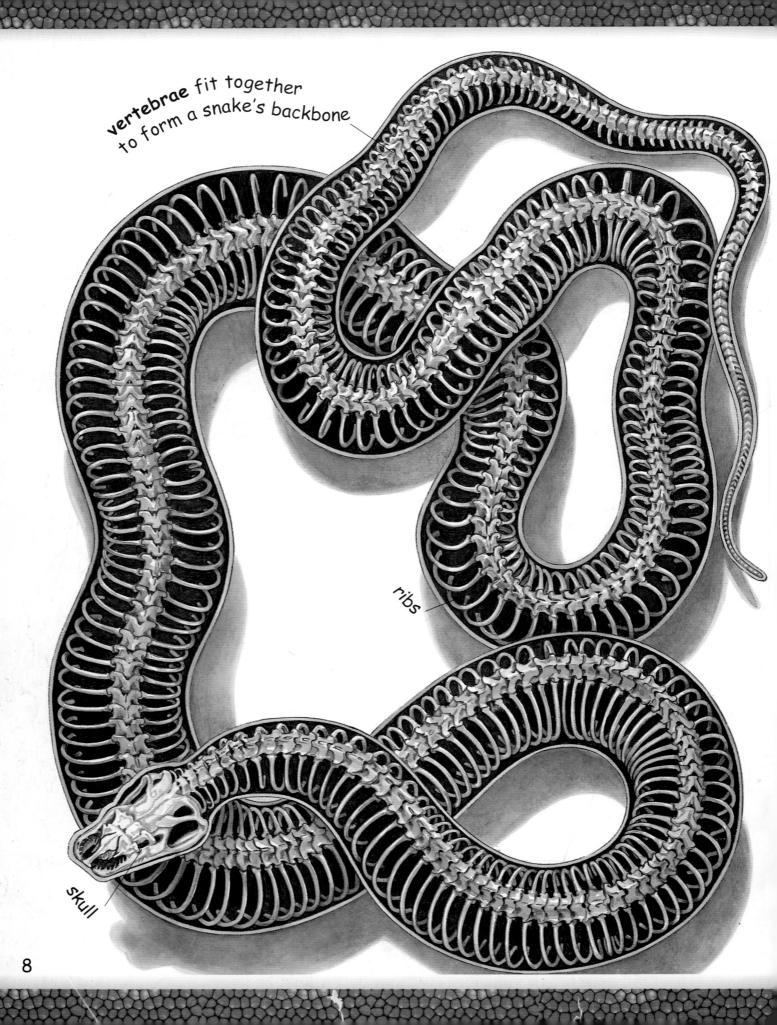

vertebrae fit together to form a snake's backbone

ribs

skull

8

What's Inside a Snake?

Snakes have long, flexible backbones and many ribs. Most snakes don't have shoulder, hip, or limb bones. Only boas and pythons have two, tiny bones that show they once had hind legs.

The ribs protect the organs inside the snake. Organs such as the kidneys are long and thin. Many snakes have one lung, not two.

long, flexible backbone

teeth

Python skull

This python's skull (left) has sharp, backward curving teeth. Teeth curved like this act as hooks to catch prey and to stop prey from escaping if it struggles.

How Do Snakes See, Hear, and Smell?

Most snakes have good eyesight.

Snakes do not have ears. They "hear" by feeling **vibrations** through the ground.

Although they have nostrils, snakes "smell" with their tongues. The tongues flick in and out of the mouth, picking up scent particles. The tips of the tongue tuck into a special organ, called Jacobson's organ, in the roof of the mouth. This "smells" the scent particles.

Cobras (below) are very poisonous. When they sense that they are threatened they defend themselves by "spitting" venom at their attacker. If the venom gets in the attacker's eye, it can cause blindness.

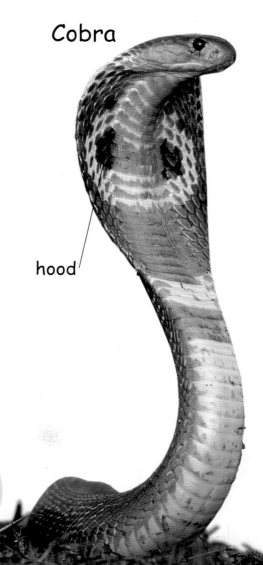

Cobra

hood

Did You Know?

A cobra "stands up" to attack its prey. Just before it strikes, special ribs swing out to support the hood, making it look even scarier.

eye

pit

Pit viper

Pit vipers (above) hunt at night. They have pits located near their eyes that sense the warmth of the animals that they hunt.

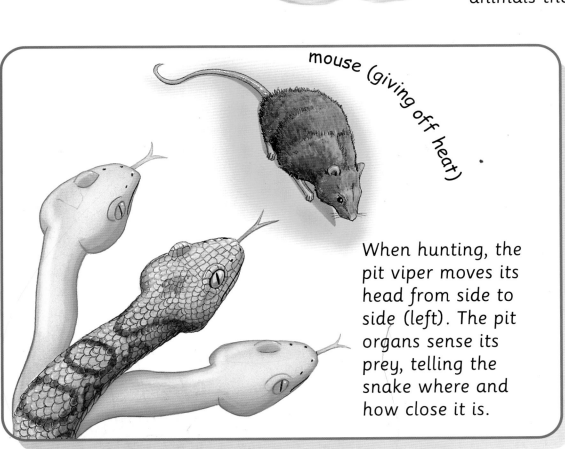

mouse (giving off heat)

When hunting, the pit viper moves its head from side to side (left). The pit organs sense its prey, telling the snake where and how close it is.

How the pit organs work

Why Do Snakes Shed Their Skin?

Hissss

Snakes cannot grow unless they shed their skin. They have to **molt**, or shed, the old outer layer regularly.

The snake stretches its jaws or rubs its mouth on something until the old skin splits. As the snake rubs more, the old skin peels off inside out.

Did You Know?

Snakes are covered in hundreds of overlapping scales, with one wide row of scales under the belly. A snake's molted skin is so thin that you can almost see through it.

Did You Know?

Snakes do not have eyelids, so they cannot shut their eyes. Each eye is protected by a tough piece of clear skin called a **spectacle**.

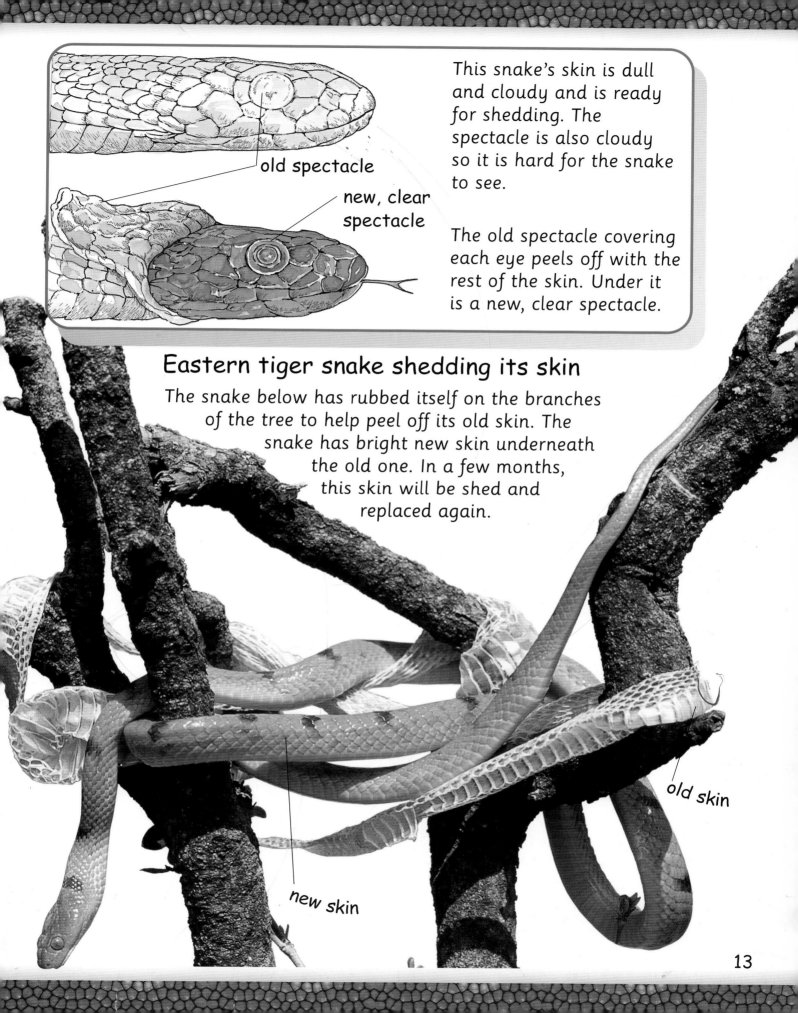

old spectacle

new, clear spectacle

This snake's skin is dull and cloudy and is ready for shedding. The spectacle is also cloudy so it is hard for the snake to see.

The old spectacle covering each eye peels off with the rest of the skin. Under it is a new, clear spectacle.

Eastern tiger snake shedding its skin

The snake below has rubbed itself on the branches of the tree to help peel off its old skin. The snake has bright new skin underneath the old one. In a few months, this skin will be shed and replaced again.

new skin

old skin

Do Snakes Get Cold?

Snakes are cold-blooded. This means they cannot control the temperature of their bodies. Their temperature is the same as the temperature of their environment. In the winter, when it gets cold outside, snakes go into a sleep-like state called **torpor**. They cannot keep themselves warm and their bodies cannot work properly in the cold.

Did You Know?

At night, when the temperature drops, snakes slow down, just as they do in winter. The next day, as it gets warmer, they wake up again, just like they do in the spring.

Rattlesnakes in a state of torpor

Puff adder basking in the Sun

If a **warm-blooded** animal gets too hot it can sweat or pant to cool itself down. Cold-blooded animals, such as snakes, cannot do this. Snakes living in very hot places spend the hottest part of the day in the shade or burrowed into the ground. If they don't stay cool, their body temperature will rise so much they will die.

In the spring, the rising temperature warms the snakes and their bodies start working again. They come out of torpor.

Are All Snakes Poisonous?

Many, but not all, snakes kill their prey by injecting it with poison called venom. Snakes attack with great speed and as their fangs enter their prey, venom is forced into the wound.

This cobra (below) is being "milked." Its venom is collected so scientists can make antivenin. Antivenin is medicine that helps people bitten by these dangerous snakes.

Fangs are large, hollow teeth in the snake's top jaw. Venom flows to the fangs from a sac in the snake's jaw.

Cobra being milked

Some snakes' venom **paralyzes** the nerves of their prey. When the prey cannot struggle any more, the snake swallows it whole.

Snake skull

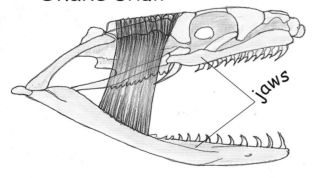

jaws

16

Spitting cobra

The Mozambique spitting cobra (above) gets its name because it can spit venom over 7 feet (2 m). It uses strong muscles to force the venom out of its fangs in two fine and deadly sprays. This means it can defend itself without getting too close to its attacker.

Did You Know?

A snake can push the end of its **trachea**, or windpipe, out of its mouth. If it couldn't do this, it would choke when it swallowed something very large.

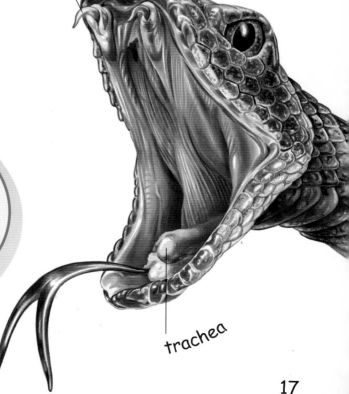

fang

trachea

17

Emerald tree boa

Are Snakes Strong?

Not all snakes kill with venom. Some snakes crush their prey to death, or squeeze them so hard that they cannot breathe. These snakes are called constrictors. They are the largest and most powerful of all snakes. Constrictors usually live in trees or by the water. They kill by looping their muscular bodies around their prey and then squeezing hard.

Did You Know?

Most snakes have only one lung, but constrictors have two, well-developed lungs. Perhaps this is because crushing prey to death uses more energy than attacking it and injecting it with venom.

Anacondas are snakes that live in South America. They can grow to be 30 feet (9 m) long and are extremely strong. They can even crush caimans to death (below). Caimans are a type of crocodile found in South America. They are very powerful and can grow to be over 7 feet (2 m) long.

anaconda

caiman

Anaconda killing a caiman

Do Snakes Lay Eggs?

Yes, many snakes lay eggs. The female lays her eggs in a safe place on the ground. The shells are tough and leathery, not hard like a chicken's egg.

Most female snakes leave their eggs once they have laid them. When they hatch, the young snakes can look after themselves.

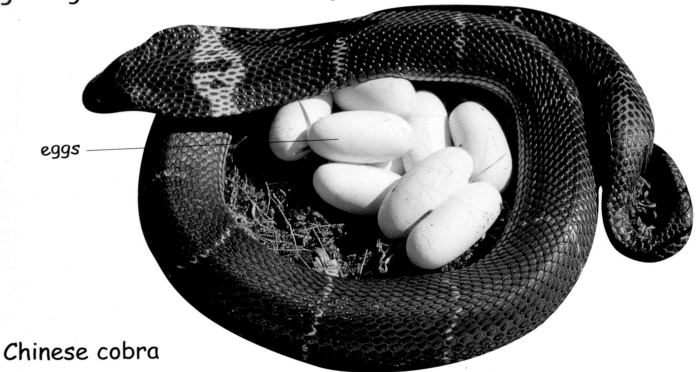

eggs

Chinese cobra

Not many snakes protect their eggs, but cobras do. This female Chinese cobra (above) has wrapped herself around her eggs to protect them. They will be safe because, like all cobras, she has deadly venom to attack enemies.

X-Ray Vision

Hold the next page up to the light and see what's inside a snake's egg.

See what's inside

leathery eggshell

baby snake hatching

amniotic fluid

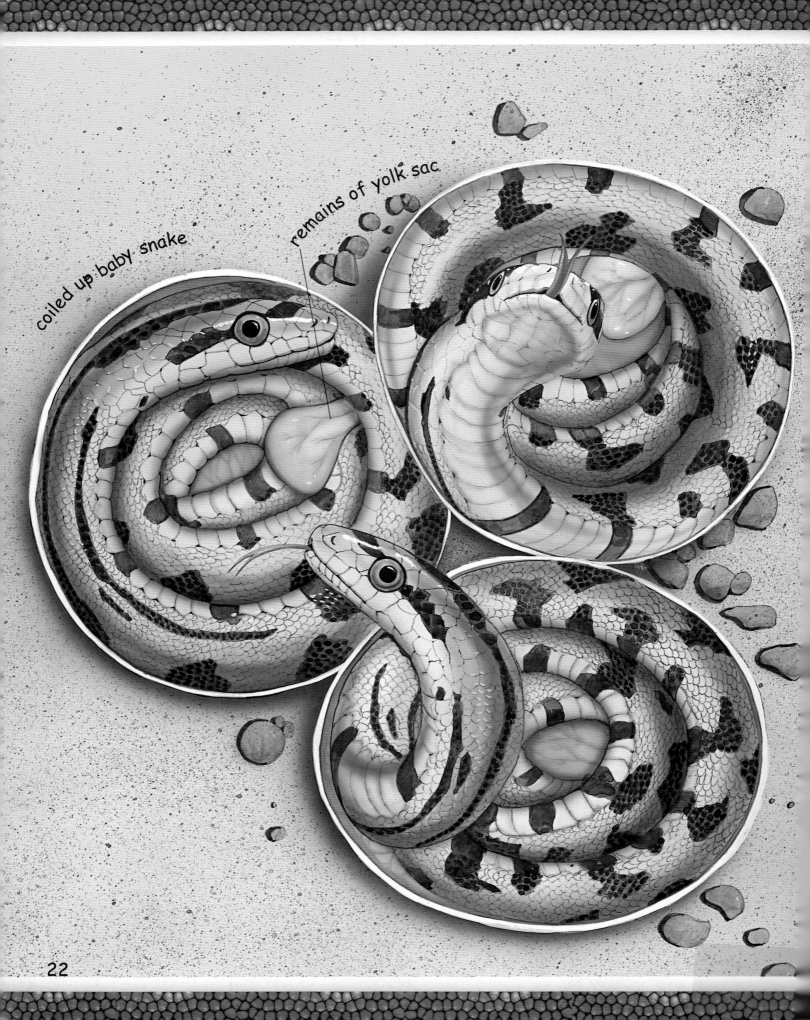

coiled up baby snake

remains of yolk sac

What Do Baby Snakes Look Like?

Inside each egg is a yolk, which is food for the baby snake.

When the baby snake eats all of the yolk, the egg hatches. The baby snake cuts the shell with a special egg tooth and comes out looking like a tiny adult. The egg tooth soon falls out.

Did You Know?

Female grass snakes lay up to 40 eggs at a time. They lay them somewhere near a compost heap, because the rotting plants keep the eggs warm and help them hatch quickly.

A special fluid, called amniotic fluid, protects everything inside the egg. As the baby snake hatches (left), the fluid appears as a lot of bubbles. It soon dries up and disappears.

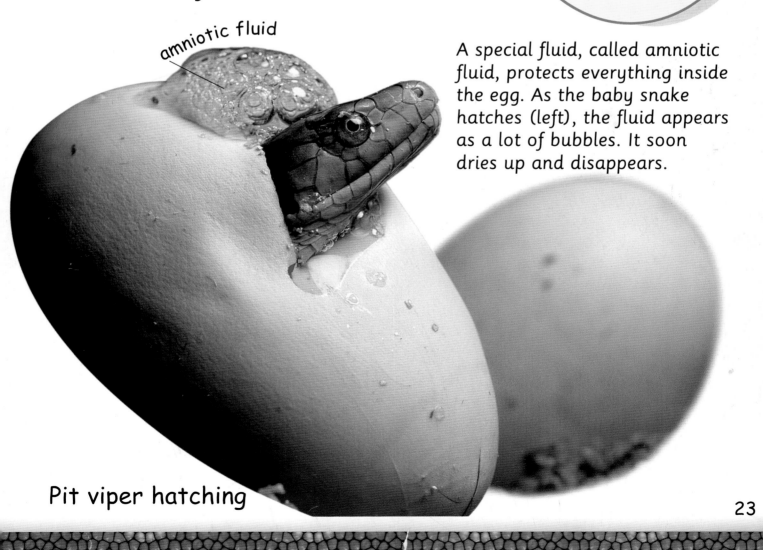

amniotic fluid

Pit viper hatching

Do Snakes Have Enemies?

Even very dangerous snakes have enemies. Snakes defend themselves in different ways. Using venom is one way, but not all snakes are poisonous. Other snakes defend themselves by hiding or escaping quickly. Some snakes look like a more dangerous type of snake than they really are.

Did You Know?

The red milk snake of North America is harmless. However, it has black and yellow bands around its body which make it look like the deadly coral snake. Scientists call it **mimicry** when a harmless animal has **evolved** to look like a more dangerous one.

Some snakes protect themselves by pretending to be dead, just like this South African ringneck spitting cobra is doing (right). It lies in an awkward twisted way with its throat showing. When the danger has passed it will quickly disappear. **Ringneck spitting cobra**

Did You Know?

The king cobra, which lives in India, Africa, and Southeast Asia, is the world's biggest poisonous snake. It can grow to 18 feet (5 m) long and its head can be as big as a human's.

One of India's most dangerous snakes is the cobra, and one of the cobra's greatest enemies is the grey mongoose. The mongoose is able to dodge the cobra's attack very quickly. This makes it a dangerous enemy.

Snakes' greatest enemy is people. Many species face **extinction** because they are hunted for their skins. Snake skins are used to make items such as the boot pictured above.

Cobra attacking mongoose

How Do Snakes Swallow Eggs?

Snakes swallow their food whole. They can't chew because their teeth are only used for holding prey or injecting venom.

Here's how the South African egg-eating snake lives up to its name. As it opens its mouth to swallow a chicken's egg, its jaws stretch apart.

Many snakes eat prey larger than themselves. They are able to do this because their jaws are fastened with a **ligament**, which stretches like elastic. The bones that hold the jaws to the skull can also move.

Did You Know?

All snakes are carnivores. They eat birds, mammals, other snakes, eggs, lizards, frogs, toads, and fish. Some of the smaller species of snakes eat insects, worms, slugs, snails, ants, and termites.

Once the snake has swallowed the egg, wave-like movements of its muscles force it along its body (below). Special "teeth," which are really parts of the neck vertebrae, slit open the egg and its contents empty into the stomach for digestion. The snake spits out the eggshell and the rest of the egg is digested.

Egg-eating snake after swallowing egg

Snakes Around the World

Snakes live in warm areas throughout the world. Because they are cold-blooded, snakes cannot live in **polar** regions like the Arctic or Antarctic, or in mountainous areas where the temperatures are low.

In the **tropics**, where it is warm all the time, snakes are active year-round.

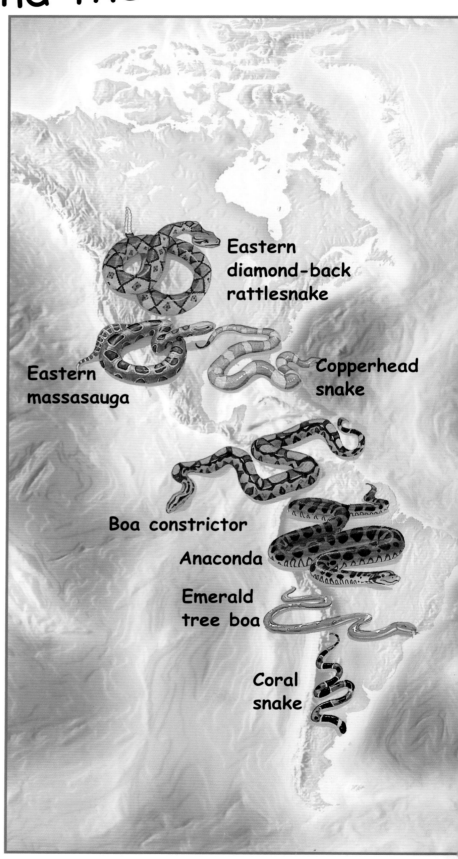

Eastern diamond-back rattlesnake

Eastern massasauga

Copperhead snake

Boa constrictor

Anaconda

Emerald tree boa

Coral snake

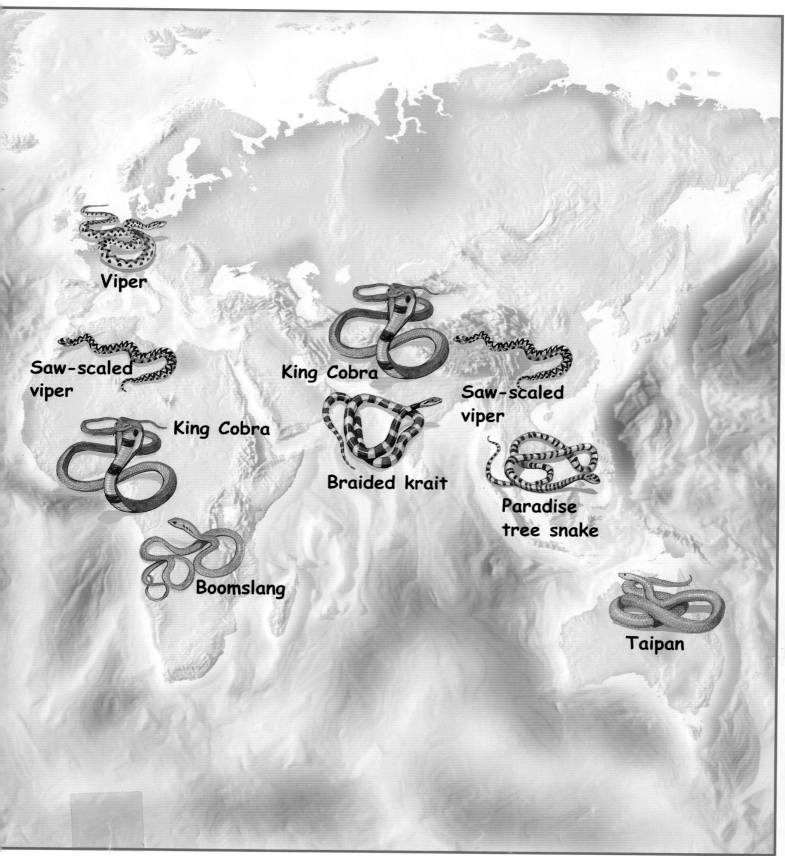

Viper

Saw-scaled viper

King Cobra

King Cobra

Braided krait

Saw-scaled viper

Boomslang

Paradise tree snake

Taipan

 # Snake Facts

The record for the longest snake in the world is held by the reticulated python. A 33 foot (10 m) long python was killed in Indonesia in 1912.

The shortest known snake is the thread snake. It is about 4 inches (10 cm) long and lives in the Caribbean.

The black mamba, found in East Africa, is the world's fastest snake. Over short distances, it can reach speeds of up to 12 mph (19 kph).

Snakes can live for a long time. In 1977, a boa constrictor at the Philadelphia Zoo died at age 40. However, wild snakes do not live as long as snakes in captivity.

The saw-scaled viper bites and kills more people each year than any other snake.

Each year, about 800 people in Sri Lanka die from snake bites.

The speed of a rattlesnake's strike is 10 feet per second (3 meters per second).

An 18 foot (5.5 m) long python has been found with a leopard in its stomach.

Snakes cause roughly 40,000 human deaths every year. About half of these occur in India.

The sea snake is the most poisonous snake on Earth. Its poison is one hundred times more deadly than any other snake's.

Snakes never stop growing, although their growth rate slows down as they get older.

The heaviest snake in the world is the anaconda. It weighs over 595 pounds (270 kg) when it is 30 feet (9 m) long.

In some parts of the world, snake charmers make snakes sway to the music of a flute. Although the snakes can hardly hear the music, they may be responding to the vibrations of the charmer's tapping foot.

The taipan is one of the world's most poisonous snakes. Although it only eats small birds and mammals, its venom sacs hold enough poison to kill up to 80 people.

 # Glossary

amphibian A cold-blooded animal that can live in water or on land but breeds in water. A frog is an amphibian.

basking Lying in the warmth of the Sun.

cold-blooded An animal whose body temperature changes according to the temperature of the air around it. A snake is cold-blooded.

evolve To develop gradually over thousands or millions of years. Through evolution, animals become better suited to their environment.

extinction When a species of plant or animal no longer exists.

gills Organs with which fish breathe.

ligament A strong, flexible, and often elastic material connecting two bones.

mimicry When an animal pretends to be another animal.

molt To shed old hair, skin, or feathers as new ones grow.

paralyze To make something unable to move or to feel anything.

polar Earth's coldest regions, north of the Arctic Circle and south of the Antarctic Circle.

prey An animal which is hunted for food by another animal.

reptile A cold-blooded animal that breathes with lungs, such as a snake or a lizard.

species A group of living things that look alike, behave in the same way, and can breed with each other.

spectacle A transparent scale that covers a snake's eye to protect it.

torpor A sluggish state that cold-blooded animals go into when the temperature drops.

trachea Another name for the windpipe, the tube in the throat through which animals breathe.

tropics The warmest parts of Earth.

venom A poison produced by some types of snake.

vertebrae The bones that make up the backbone.

vibrations Very small movements that can sometimes be felt through the ground.

warm-blooded An animal whose temperature remains almost the same, whatever the temperature around it.

Index